THE BEGINNER'S GUIDE TO SEO

BOOST YOUR WEBSITE'S VISIBILITY

Acknowledgement

I would like to express my deepest gratitude to my parents, whose unwavering love, encouragement, and support have been the cornerstone of my journey.

I am also immensely thankful to my company, Socialight, for providing me with invaluable opportunities to grow and thrive in the dynamic field of digital marketing. The exposure I have gained here has been instrumental in shaping my skills and broadening my perspective.

Special thanks are due to our esteemed CEO, Tarun Kumar, whose visionary leadership, and unwavering commitment to excellence have been a constant source of inspiration. Under his guidance, I have gained practical exposure and insights that have not only enriched my professional growth but also motivated me to push my limits and strive for greatness.

To everyone who has contributed to my personal and professional growth, whether through mentorship, collaboration, or support, I extend my heartfelt thanks. Your belief in me has been instrumental in my success, and I am truly grateful for the impact you have had on my journey.

Table of Contents

Introduction

Welcome to the world of SEO! In today's digital age, where billions of searches are conducted every day, having a solid understanding of Search Engine Optimization (SEO) is essential for anyone with an online presence. Whether you're a business owner, a blogger, or a website developer, mastering the fundamentals of SEO can significantly impact your website's visibility and success.

"Think of SEO as a road map for your website. Just like a map helps travelers navigate through unfamiliar territory, SEO guides internet users to your website amidst the vast online landscape."

Why SEO matters for your website

SEO is the process of optimizing your website to rank higher in search engine results pages (SERPs) and attract more organic (non-paid) traffic. When your website appears at the top of search results for relevant queries, you are more likely to receive clicks, visits, and potential customers. In essence, SEO is the bridge that connects your website to its audience, driving targeted traffic and increasing your online visibility.

What to expect from this Book

In this comprehensive Beginner's Guide to SEO, we will take you on a journey through the fundamental principles and strategies of search engine optimization. From understanding the basics of SEO to implementing advanced techniques, this Book will equip you with the knowledge and tools necessary to boost your website's visibility and attract more organic traffic.

Throughout this guide, we will cover everything you need to know to get started with SEO, including:

1. **Understanding SEO Basics:** We will break down the fundamentals of SEO, including what it is, why it matters, and how search engines work.
2. **Keyword Research and Analysis:** Learn how to identify the right keywords for your website and leverage them to improve your search engine rankings.
3. **On-Page SEO Optimization:** Discover techniques for optimizing your website's on-page

elements, such as meta tags, headers, and content, to enhance its visibility in search results.

4. **Off-Page SEO Strategies:** Explore strategies for building backlinks, leveraging social media, and implementing local SEO tactics to strengthen your website's authority and relevance.

5. **Technical SEO Fundamentals:** Learn about technical aspects of SEO, including website speed optimization, mobile optimization, and structured data markup, to ensure your site is easily accessible and indexable by search engines.

6. **Measuring Success with SEO Metrics:** Discover key performance indicators (KPIs) for SEO and learn how to track and analyze your website's performance using various analytics tools.

7. **Common SEO Mistakes to Avoid:** Learn about common pitfalls to avoid in SEO, such as keyword stuffing, ignoring mobile optimization, and failing to keep up with algorithm updates.

8. **Advanced SEO Techniques:** Delve into advanced SEO techniques, including schema markup implementation, advanced link-building

strategies, and voice search optimization, to take your SEO efforts to the next level.

In conclusion, this Book is designed to provide you with a comprehensive understanding of SEO and empower you to optimize your website effectively. Whether you are a beginner looking to get started or an experienced marketer seeking to refine your strategies, this guide has something for everyone.

Chapter 1: Understanding SEO Basics

"Imagine your website as a shop in a bustling marketplace. SEO is like signage and advertising that directs customers to your shop, ensuring it stands out among the competition."

Search Engine Optimization (SEO) is a crucial component of digital marketing, aimed at improving a website's visibility in search engine results pages (SERPs). In this chapter, we will explore the fundamental concepts of SEO, including its definition, significance, and the mechanisms behind search engines.

What is SEO?

SEO encompasses a set of strategies and techniques designed to optimize a website's content, structure, and other elements to increase its visibility and organic (non-paid) traffic from search engines like Google, Bing, and Yahoo. The goal of SEO is to improve a website's ranking in relevant search queries, thereby driving more targeted traffic and potential customers.

SEO involves various tactics, including keyword research, on-page optimization, link building, and technical optimization. These strategies aim to make a website more accessible, relevant, and authoritative in the eyes of search engines, ultimately improving its chances of ranking higher in search results.

Why is SEO important for websites?

SEO is essential for websites for several reasons:

1. **Increased Visibility:** Most online experiences begin with a search engine, making it crucial for websites to appear prominently in search results. By optimizing for relevant keywords, websites can improve their visibility and attract more organic traffic.

2. **Higher Quality Traffic:** Unlike paid advertising, which targets users based on demographics or interests, organic search traffic consists of users actively seeking information or solutions related to their search queries. As a result, organic traffic tends to be more relevant and of higher

quality, leading to better engagement and conversion rates.

3. **Cost-Effectiveness:** While paid advertising can yield immediate results, it requires ongoing investment and can be costly in the long run. SEO, on the other hand, offers a cost-effective way to attract organic traffic over time, providing a sustainable source of leads and customers without ongoing advertising expenses.

4. **Credibility and Trust:** Websites that rank higher in search results are often perceived as more credible and trustworthy by users. By optimizing for SEO, websites can improve their authority and reputation in their respective industries, enhancing user trust and confidence.

5. **Competitive Advantage:** In today's competitive digital landscape, SEO can provide a significant competitive advantage. Websites that invest in SEO are more likely to outrank their competitors in search results, gaining a larger share of organic traffic and potential customers.

How search engines work

Search engines like Google use complex algorithms to crawl, index, and rank billions of web pages based on their relevance and authority. Here is a simplified overview of how search engines work:

1. **Crawling:** Search engines deploy automated bots called crawlers or spiders to systematically browse the web and discover new web pages. These crawlers follow links from one page to another, indexing the content of each page they encounter.

2. **Indexing:** Once a web page is crawled, its content is analyzed and indexed in the search

engine's database. During indexing, search engines extract key information from the page, including its text, images, and metadata, to determine its relevance to specific search queries.

3. **Ranking:** When a user enters a search query, the search engine retrieves relevant web pages from its index and ranks them based on various factors, including relevance, authority, and user experience. Pages that are deemed most relevant and authoritative for the search query are displayed at the top of the search results.

Search engine algorithms consider hundreds of factors when determining rankings, including keyword relevance, backlink quality, user engagement metrics, and website speed. By understanding how search engines work and optimizing their websites accordingly, webmasters can improve their chances of ranking higher in search results and attracting more organic traffic.

In the following chapters, we will delve deeper into the key strategies and techniques of SEO, exploring how to conduct keyword research, optimize on-page elements, build high-quality backlinks, and measure SEO performance. By mastering the fundamentals of SEO, you will be well-equipped to boost your website's visibility and achieve your digital marketing goals.

Chapter 2: Keyword Research and Analysis

"Picture your website as a library. Keywords are like index cards that help visitors find the books they are looking for. Conducting keyword research is akin to organizing these cards efficiently to improve accessibility."

In the vast landscape of Search Engine Optimization (SEO), keywords reign supreme. Understanding the importance of keywords in SEO, learning how to conduct keyword research effectively, and utilizing tools for keyword analysis are critical steps toward boosting your website's visibility. In this chapter, we will delve into these essential aspects of keyword research and analysis.

Importance of Keywords in SEO

Keywords act as the guiding stars that lead search engine users to your website. They are the phrases and terms users type into search engines to find information, products, or services. Here's why keywords are crucial in SEO:

1. **Relevance:** By incorporating relevant keywords into your website's content, you signal to search engines what your website is about, increasing its relevance for specific search queries.
2. **Visibility:** Ranking for relevant keywords ensures that your website appears prominently in search engine results pages (SERPs), increasing its visibility to potential visitors.
3. **User Intent:** Understanding the intent behind search queries helps you create content that addresses the needs and interests of your target audience, leading to better user engagement and satisfaction.
4. **Competitive Advantage:** Effective keyword optimization allows you to outrank competitors in search results, attracting more organic traffic and potential customers to your website.

How to Conduct Keyword Research

Keyword research is the process of identifying the words and phrases your target audience is using in search queries. Here is a step-by-step guide to conducting keyword research, illustrated with examples:

1. **Identify Seed Keywords:** Start by brainstorming a list of seed keywords that are relevant to your website's content or niche. These are broad terms that describe your products, services, or topics.

   For example, if you run a pet grooming business, your seed keywords might include "dog grooming," "cat grooming," and "pet grooming services."

2. **Expand Your Keyword List:** Use keyword research tools to expand your list of keywords and uncover new opportunities. Tools like Google Keyword Planner, SEMrush, or Ahrefs can provide valuable insights into keyword search volume, competition, and related terms.

   For instance, when researching the keyword "dog grooming," you might discover related terms such as "dog grooming near me," "dog grooming tips," and "dog grooming supplies."

3. **Consider Long-Tail Keywords:** Long-tail keywords are longer, more specific phrases that typically have lower search volume but higher conversion rates. These keywords can help you attract highly targeted traffic to your website.

   For example, "professional dog grooming services in [your city]" or "best cat grooming techniques for long-haired breeds."

4. **Evaluate Keyword Difficulty and Search Volume:** Assess the competition and search volume for each keyword to determine its potential value. Look for keywords with a balance of reasonable competition and sufficient search volume. Tools like SEMrush and Ahrefs provide metrics such as keyword difficulty scores and search volume estimates to help you make informed decisions.

5. **Refine Your Keyword List:** Refine your keyword list based on relevance, search volume, and competition. Focus on selecting keywords that align with your website's content, target

audience, and goals. You may also prioritize keywords with high commercial intent or informational value, depending on your business objectives.

Tools for Keyword Analysis

Several tools are available to assist you in analyzing keywords and optimizing your website's content. Here are some essential tools for keyword analysis:

1. **Google Keyword Planner:** Google's free keyword research tool provides insights into keyword search volume, competition, and suggested bid prices for paid advertising. It is an excellent starting point for beginners and integrates seamlessly with Google Ads.

2. **SEMrush:** SEMrush offers comprehensive keyword research features, including keyword suggestions, search volume data, keyword difficulty scores, and competitor analysis. It provides valuable insights into your competitors' keyword strategies and helps identify keyword opportunities in your niche.

3. **Ahrefs:** Ahrefs is a powerful SEO tool that offers advanced keyword research capabilities, backlink analysis, and site auditing features. It provides detailed keyword metrics, including search volume, keyword difficulty, and SERP features, allowing you to identify high-potential keywords and track their performance over time.

4. **Moz Keyword Explorer:** Moz's keyword research tool provides valuable insights into keyword opportunities, including search volume, keyword difficulty, and organic click-through rates. It offers actionable recommendations for optimizing your website's content and improving its search engine rankings.

By leveraging these tools and following best practices for keyword research, you can identify high-potential keywords, optimize your website's content effectively, and improve its visibility in search engine results pages (SERPs). In the next chapter, we will explore strategies for optimizing your website's on-page elements, including page titles, meta descriptions, and headers, to further enhance its visibility and relevance in search results.

Chapter 3: On-Page SEO Optimization

"Consider your website as a book. On-page SEO optimization is like polishing the cover, ensuring it is attractive and informative, enticing readers to delve deeper into the content."

In this chapter, we will delve into the essential aspects of on-page SEO optimization, including optimizing page titles, meta descriptions, and headers, creating high-quality content, and understanding the importance of user experience (UX) in SEO.

Optimizing Page Titles, Meta Descriptions, and Headers

1. **Page Titles (Character Limit: 50-60 characters)**
   Page titles are crucial for both search engine optimization and user engagement. They appear as the clickable headline in search engine results pages (SERPs) and should accurately

reflect the content of the page while incorporating relevant keywords.

Example: For a pet grooming website, a well-optimized page title could be: "Professional Dog Grooming Services | Pamper Your Pooch Today"

2. **Meta Descriptions (Character Limit: 150-160 characters)**

Meta descriptions provide a brief summary of the page's content and play a significant role in influencing click-through rates from search results. They should be descriptive, compelling, and include relevant keywords to entice users to click.

Example: "Discover our range of professional dog grooming services tailored to your pet's needs. From baths to haircuts, we'll keep your furry friend looking their best."

3. **Headers (Character Limit: No strict limit, but keep them concise)**

Headers (H1, H2, H3, etc.) help structure and organize content on a web page. They should be used to break up content into logical sections and provide hierarchy. Incorporate relevant keywords into headers to improve SEO. Example:

- H1: "Expert Dog Grooming Tips for Pet Owners"
- H2: "Choosing the Right Grooming Products"
- H3: "Tips for Dealing with Shedding"

Creating High-Quality Content

High-quality content is the cornerstone of on-page SEO optimization. It should be valuable, relevant, and engaging to users while incorporating targeted keywords naturally. Here are some tips for creating high-quality content:

1. **Relevance:** Ensure that your content is relevant to your target audience and addresses their needs or interests. Conduct keyword research to identify relevant topics and incorporate targeted keywords throughout your content.

2. **Value:** Provide valuable information, insights, or solutions that meet the needs of your audience. Offer unique perspectives, actionable advice, or in-depth analysis that sets your content apart from competitors.

3. **Engagement:** Create content that encourages user engagement and interaction. Use multimedia elements such as images, videos, and infographics to enhance readability and appeal.

Understanding the Importance of User Experience (UX) in SEO

User experience (UX) plays a critical role in on-page SEO optimization. Search engines prioritize websites that deliver positive user experiences, as reflected in metrics such as bounce rate and time on page. Here's why UX is essential in SEO:

1. **Accessibility**: Ensure that your website is accessible to all users, including those with disabilities or using assistive technologies. Use clear navigation, readable fonts, and descriptive alt text for images to enhance accessibility.

2. **Mobile-Friendliness:** With the increasing use of mobile devices for internet browsing, mobile-friendliness is crucial for SEO. Optimize your website for mobile devices, including responsive design, fast load times, and mobile-friendly navigation.

3. **Site Speed:** Page speed is a significant factor in both user experience and SEO. Ensure that your website loads quickly on all devices to prevent user frustration and improve search engine rankings.

Incorporating on-page SEO optimization techniques, such as optimizing page titles, meta descriptions, and headers, creating high-quality content, and prioritizing user experience, can significantly improve your website's visibility and rankings in search engine results pages (SERPs). In the next chapter, we will explore off-page SEO strategies, including building backlinks, leveraging social media, and optimizing for local search, to further enhance your website's online presence and authority.

Chapter 4: Off-Page SEO Strategies

"Think of your website as a social gathering. Off-page SEO strategies are akin to networking and building relationships with others in the community, increasing your website's reputation and credibility."

Off-page SEO strategies are essential for enhancing your website's authority, credibility, and visibility in search engine results pages (SERPs). In this chapter, we will explore three key off-page SEO tactics: building backlinks, leveraging social media, and implementing local SEO tactics.

Building Backlinks

Backlinks, also known as inbound links, are links from other websites that point to your website. They play a crucial role in off-page SEO as they signal to search engines that your website is authoritative and trustworthy. Here is how to build backlinks effectively:

1. **Create High-Quality Content:** The best way to attract backlinks is to create valuable, informative, and engaging content that others want to link to. Focus on producing content that fills a gap in the market, provides unique insights, or solves a problem for your target audience.

2. **Reach Out to Influencers and Websites:** Identify influencers, bloggers, and websites in your niche and reach out to them to promote your content. Offer to write guest posts, contribute to round-up articles, or collaborate on content projects that provide value to their audience.

3. **Submit to Directories and Resource Pages:** Submit your website to relevant directories and resource pages in your industry. Look for authoritative directories and niche-specific resource pages that allow you to include a link back to your website.

4. **Monitor and Disavow Toxic Backlinks:** Regularly monitor your backlink profile using tools like Google Search Console or Ahrefs. Identify any low-quality or spammy backlinks and disavow them to prevent them from harming your website's reputation.

Social Media and Its Impact on SEO

While social media signals themselves do not directly impact search engine rankings, social media can indirectly influence your website's SEO in several ways:

1. **Increased Brand Visibility:** Active participation on social media platforms can increase your brand's visibility and reach, leading to more brand mentions, shares, and engagement, which can indirectly contribute to improved SEO.

2. **Content Promotion:** Social media provides an effective platform for promoting your content and driving traffic back to your website. Share your blog posts, articles, videos, and other content on social media channels to attract visitors and potential backlinks.

3. **Social Signals:** Although not a direct ranking factor, social signals such as likes, shares, comments, and retweets can indicate the popularity and relevance of your content, which may indirectly influence search engine rankings.

4. **Local SEO Benefits:** Social media profiles often rank well in local search results. Optimizing your social media profiles with accurate business information, including your location, can improve your visibility in local search results.

Local SEO Tactics

Local SEO focuses on optimizing your website to attract local customers and improve your visibility in local search results. Here are some key local SEO tactics to consider:

1. **Optimize Google My Business:** Claim and optimize your Google My Business listing with

accurate business information, including your name, address, phone number, and business hours. Encourage customers to leave reviews and respond to reviews promptly.

Yashoda Hospitals - Somajiguda
4.8 ★ ★ ★ ★ ★ 25,591 Google reviews ⋮
Private hospital in Hyderabad, Telangana

◎ Website   ◈ Directions   ⬚ Save   ☎ Call

Address: 6-3-905, Raj Bhavan Rd, Matha Nagar, Somajiguda, Hyderabad, Telangana 500082
Phone: 063669 20627
Hours: Open 24 hours ▾

2. **Local Keyword Optimization:** Use local keywords in your website content, meta tags, and headings to target local search queries. Include location-specific terms such as city names, neighborhoods, and landmarks relevant to your target audience.

3. **Local Citations and Directories:** Ensure that your business is listed accurately in online

directories, review sites, and local citation sources such as Yelp, TripAdvisor, and Yellow Pages. Consistent NAP (Name, Address, Phone Number) information across all listings is crucial for local SEO.

4. **Localized Content:** Create content tailored to your local audience, such as blog posts, articles, or events related to your community or industry. Highlight local news, events, and landmarks to demonstrate your relevance to local searchers.

By implementing these off-page SEO strategies, including building high-quality backlinks, leveraging social media, and optimizing for local search, you can enhance your website's authority, visibility, and relevance in search engine results pages (SERPs). In the next chapter, we will explore technical SEO fundamentals, including website speed optimization, mobile optimization, and structured data markup, to further improve your website's SEO performance.

Chapter 5: Technical SEO Fundamentals

"Envision your website as a house. Technical SEO is like maintaining the infrastructure - ensuring the foundation is strong, the rooms are well-lit and spacious, and the pathways are clear and easy to navigate."

Technical SEO focuses on optimizing the technical aspects of your website to improve its visibility and performance in search engine results pages (SERPs). In this chapter, we will explore three key technical SEO fundamentals: website speed optimization, mobile optimization, and structured data markup.

Website Speed Optimization

Website speed, also known as page load time, is a critical factor in both user experience and search engine rankings. Slow-loading websites can frustrate users and lead to higher bounce rates, negatively impacting your website's SEO. Here is how to optimize website speed:

1. **Minimize HTTP Requests:** Reduce the number of HTTP requests by minimizing the use of external scripts, stylesheets, and images. Combine multiple files into one where possible to reduce server requests.

2. **Optimize Images:** Compress images to reduce file size without sacrificing quality. Use image compression tools and formats like JPEG or WebP to optimize images for the web.

3. **Enable Browser Caching:** Enable browser caching to store static files (e.g., images, CSS, JavaScript) locally on users' devices, reducing the need for repeated downloads and speeding up page load times for returning visitors.

4. **Reduce Server Response Time:** Improve server response time by optimizing server configurations, upgrading hosting plans, and implementing caching mechanisms such as Content Delivery Networks (CDNs) to serve content from servers closer to users.

5. **Minimize Redirects and Eliminate Render-Blocking Resources:** Minimize the use of redirects and eliminate render-blocking resources (e.g., JavaScript and CSS files) that

delay page rendering. Optimize critical rendering paths to ensure faster loading times.

Mobile Optimization

With the increasing prevalence of mobile devices, mobile optimization is essential for both user experience and SEO. Google prioritizes mobile-friendly websites in its search results, making mobile optimization a crucial aspect of technical SEO. Here is how to optimize your website for mobile:

1. Use Responsive Design: Implement responsive web design to ensure that your website adapts seamlessly to different screen sizes and devices. A responsive design provides a consistent user experience across desktops, tablets, and smartphones.

2. Optimize Page Load Times: Mobile users expect fast-loading pages. Apply the same speed optimization techniques mentioned earlier to improve page load times on mobile devices.

3. Optimize Touch Elements: Ensure that touch elements such as buttons, links, and navigation menus are large enough and spaced appropriately for easy tapping on touch screens.

Optimize form fields for mobile input to enhance usability.

4. Prioritize Mobile Content: Prioritize content that is relevant and useful to mobile users. Condense lengthy content, prioritize key information, and optimize images and multimedia for mobile viewing.

5. Test and Monitor Performance: Regularly test your website's mobile performance using tools like Google's Mobile-Friendly Test and PageSpeed Insights. Monitor mobile-specific metrics such as mobile traffic, bounce rates, and conversion rates to identify areas for improvement.

Structured Data Markup

Structured data markup, also known as schema markup, is a standardized format for providing additional context and metadata to search engines about the content of web pages. Implementing structured data markup can enhance search engine visibility and improve the display of your website's snippets in SERPs. Here is how to implement structured data markup:

1. **Identify Relevant Schema Types:** Determine which schema types are relevant to your website's content and objectives. Common schema types include organization, product, article, event, and local business.

2. **Implement Schema Markup:** Add structured data markup to your website's HTML code using Schema.org vocabulary. Markup elements such as JSON-LD, Microdata, or RDFa can be used to annotate specific pieces of content with schema properties.

3. **Test Structured Data:** Use Google's Structured Data Testing Tool or Rich Results Test to validate your structured data markup and ensure that it is implemented correctly. Address any errors or warnings identified during testing.

4. **Monitor Rich Results:** Monitor your website's performance in search results and track the appearance of rich results, such as rich snippets, rich cards, and knowledge panels. Monitor changes in click-through rates and traffic resulting from the implementation of structured data markup.

By implementing these technical SEO fundamentals, including website speed optimization, mobile optimization, and structured data markup, you can enhance your website's performance, usability, and visibility in search engine results pages (SERPs). In the next chapter, we will explore how to measure success with SEO metrics and track the performance of your SEO efforts using key performance indicators (KPIs) and analytics tools.

Chapter 6: Measuring Success with SEO Metrics

"Think of your website as a garden. SEO metrics are like tools that help you measure the health and growth of your plants. By analyzing these metrics, you can identify areas for improvement and cultivate a thriving garden."

In this chapter, we will explore how to measure the success of your SEO efforts using key performance indicators (KPIs), tools for tracking and analyzing SEO performance, and how to interpret analytics data effectively.

Key Performance Indicators (KPIs) for SEO

Key performance indicators (KPIs) are metrics used to evaluate the effectiveness and performance of your SEO strategies. By tracking these KPIs, you can assess the impact of your efforts and make data-driven decisions to optimize your SEO strategy. Here are some essential KPIs for SEO:

1. **Organic Traffic:** Organic traffic refers to the number of visitors who find your website through organic search results. Monitoring organic traffic allows you to gauge the overall performance of your SEO efforts and track changes over time.

2. **Keyword Rankings:** Tracking keyword rankings helps you understand how well your website is performing for specific search queries. Monitor the rankings of your target keywords in search engine results pages (SERPs) to identify trends and opportunities for improvement.

3. **Click-Through Rate (CTR):** CTR measures the percentage of users who click on your website's link in search results after seeing it. A high CTR indicates that your titles and meta descriptions are compelling and relevant to users' search queries.

4. **Conversion Rate:** Conversion rate measures the percentage of website visitors who complete a desired action, such as making a purchase, filling out a form, or signing up for a newsletter. Tracking conversion rates helps you assess the effectiveness of your SEO in driving valuable actions.

5. **Bounce Rate:** Bounce rate refers to the percentage of visitors who navigate away from your website after viewing only one page. A high bounce rate may indicate poor user experience or irrelevant content.

6. **Backlink Profile:** Monitoring your backlink profile allows you to track the quantity and quality of inbound links pointing to your website. A healthy backlink profile with high-quality, relevant links can improve your website's authority and rankings.

Tools for Tracking and Analyzing SEO Performance

Several tools are available to help you track and analyze your website's SEO performance. These tools provide valuable insights into key metrics, competitor analysis, keyword research, and more. Here are some essential tools for tracking and analyzing SEO performance:

1. **Google Analytics:** Google Analytics is a free web analytics tool that provides detailed insights into website traffic, user behavior, and conversion metrics. It allows you to track organic traffic, keyword performance, and other key SEO metrics.

2. **Google Search Console:** Google Search Console is a free tool provided by Google that helps you monitor and maintain your website's presence in Google Search results. It provides valuable data on search performance, indexing status, and site errors.

3. **SEMrush:** SEMrush is a comprehensive SEO toolkit that offers features such as keyword research, backlink analysis, site auditing, and

competitor analysis. It provides valuable insights into keyword rankings, traffic trends, and opportunities for optimization.

4. **Ahrefs:** Ahrefs is a powerful SEO toolset that offers features such as keyword research, backlink analysis, site auditing, and rank tracking. It provides in-depth insights into your website's backlink profile, keyword rankings, and competitor analysis.

5. **Moz Pro:** Moz Pro offers a suite of SEO tools for keyword research, rank tracking, site auditing, and link analysis. It provides valuable insights into your website's performance and opportunities for improvement.

Interpreting Analytics Data

Interpreting analytics data is crucial for understanding the effectiveness of your SEO efforts and identifying areas for improvement. Here are some tips for interpreting analytics data effectively:

1. **Set Goals:** Define clear goals and objectives for your SEO efforts, such as increasing organic traffic, improving keyword rankings, or driving

conversions. Use analytics data to track progress toward these goals.

2. **Monitor Trends:** Look for trends and patterns in your analytics data over time. Monitor changes in organic traffic, keyword rankings, and other metrics to identify opportunities and potential issues.

3. **Compare Performance:** Compare your website's performance to industry benchmarks and competitor data to assess your relative performance and identify areas where you can improve.

4. **Identify Opportunities:** Use analytics data to identify opportunities for optimization and improvement. Look for keywords with high search volume and low competition, pages with high bounce rates, or untapped market segments.

5. **Take Action:** Use insights from analytics data to inform your SEO strategy and make data-driven decisions. Implement changes, experiments, and optimizations based on analytics data to improve your website's performance over time.

By tracking key performance indicators (KPIs), leveraging tools for tracking, and analyzing SEO performance, and interpreting analytics data effectively, you can measure the success of your SEO efforts and make informed decisions to optimize your website's visibility and performance in search engine results pages (SERPs). In the next chapter, we will explore common SEO mistakes to avoid to ensure the effectiveness of your SEO strategy.

Chapter 7: Common SEO Mistakes to Avoid

"Imagine your website as a vehicle on a long journey. Avoiding common SEO mistakes is like performing regular maintenance on your vehicle, ensuring it runs smoothly and efficiently without any breakdowns along the way."

In this chapter, we will explore some common SEO mistakes that beginners often make and provide guidance on how to avoid them to ensure the effectiveness of your SEO strategy.

Keyword Stuffing and Other Black Hat Tactics

Keyword stuffing is the practice of excessively and unnaturally using keywords throughout your website's content in an attempt to manipulate search engine rankings. While keywords are essential for SEO, overusing them can lead to a poor user experience and result in penalties from search engines. Here is how to avoid keyword stuffing and other black hat tactics:

1. **Focus on Quality Content:** Instead of obsessing over keyword density, prioritize creating high-quality, valuable content that is relevant to your audience. Write naturally and incorporate keywords in a way that feels organic and adds value to the user experience.

2. **Use Keywords Strategically:** Identify target keywords for each page of your website and incorporate them naturally into titles, headings, body text, and meta tags. Aim for a balance between optimization for search engines and readability for users.

3. **Avoid Over-Optimization:** Be cautious of over-optimizing your content by cramming too many keywords into your copy. Instead, prioritize user intent and readability, and let keywords naturally flow within the context of your content.

4. **Diversify Anchor Text:** When building backlinks, avoid using exact-match anchor text excessively. Instead, use a variety of anchor text variations and natural language to create a diverse and natural-looking link profile.

Ignoring Mobile Optimization

With the increasing prevalence of mobile devices for internet browsing, mobile optimization is essential for SEO success. Ignoring mobile optimization can result in poor user experience, decreased engagement, and lower search engine rankings. Here is how to avoid ignoring mobile optimization:

1. **Implement Responsive Design:** Ensure that your website is responsive and adapts seamlessly to different screen sizes and devices. Responsive design provides a consistent user experience across desktops, tablets, and smartphones.

2. **Optimize Page Load Times:** Mobile users expect fast-loading pages. Optimize your website's performance for mobile devices by minimizing page load times, optimizing images, and leveraging browser caching techniques.

3. **Prioritize Mobile-Friendly Features:** Prioritize mobile-friendly features such as touch-friendly navigation, legible font sizes, and clear calls-to-action. Make it easy for mobile users to navigate your website and access important information.

4. **Test Across Devices:** Regularly test your website across various devices and screen sizes to ensure compatibility and functionality. Use tools like Google's Mobile-Friendly Test to identify and address any mobile usability issues.

Not Keeping Up with Algorithm Updates

Search engine algorithms are constantly evolving to provide more relevant and useful search results to users. Not keeping up with algorithm updates can result in your website losing visibility and rankings in search engine results pages (SERPs). Here is how to avoid falling behind on algorithm updates:

1. **Stay Informed:** Stay updated on the latest SEO news and algorithm updates by following reputable industry blogs, forums, and official announcements from search engines like Google.
2. **Adapt and Adjust:** Be prepared to adapt your SEO strategy in response to algorithm updates. Monitor changes in your website's rankings and

traffic, and adjust your tactics accordingly to maintain or improve performance.

3. **Focus on User Experience:** Many algorithm updates prioritize user experience factors such as page speed, mobile-friendliness, and content quality. By prioritizing user experience in your SEO strategy, you can future-proof your website against algorithm changes.

4. **Diversify Your Strategy:** Instead of relying on a single SEO tactic or strategy, diversify your approach to include a mix of on-page optimization, content creation, link building, and technical SEO. A well-rounded strategy is more resilient to algorithm updates.

By avoiding common SEO mistakes such as keyword stuffing, ignoring mobile optimization, and not keeping up with algorithm updates, you can ensure the effectiveness and longevity of your SEO efforts. In the next chapter, we will explore advanced SEO techniques that can further enhance your website's visibility and performance in search engine results pages (SERPs).

Chapter 8: Advanced SEO Techniques

"Consider your website as a skilled athlete. Advanced SEO techniques are like specialized training exercises that push your website's performance to the next level, helping it outperform competitors and achieve peak visibility."

In this chapter, we will explore advanced SEO techniques that can take your website's visibility and performance to the next level. These techniques go beyond the basics and require a deeper understanding of SEO principles and strategies.

Schema Markup Implementation

Schema markup, also known as structured data markup, is a type of code that helps search engines understand the content and context of your web pages more effectively. By implementing schema markup, you can enhance your website's appearance in search engine results pages (SERPs) and provide users with more relevant and informative snippets. Here is how to implement schema markup effectively:

1. **Identify Relevant Schema Types:** Determine which types of schema markup are most relevant to your website's content and objectives. Common schema types include organization, product, article, event, and local business.

2. **Implement Schema Markup:** Add structured data markup to your website's HTML code using Schema.org vocabulary. Markup elements such as JSON-LD, Microdata, or RDFa can be used to annotate specific pieces of content with schema properties.

3. **Optimize for Rich Snippets:** Implement schema markup to optimize your website for rich snippets, which are enhanced search results that include additional information such as star ratings, reviews, and event details. Optimizing for rich snippets can improve your website's visibility and click-through rates in SERPs.

4. **Test and Validate Markup:** Use tools like Google's Structured Data Testing Tool or Rich Results Test to validate your schema markup

and ensure that it is implemented correctly. Address any errors or warnings identified during testing to maximize the effectiveness of your markup.

Advanced Link-Building Strategies

Link building is a critical aspect of SEO that involves acquiring backlinks from other websites to improve your website's authority and credibility. Advanced link-building strategies go beyond basic tactics and focus on building high-quality, relevant links that drive organic traffic and improve search engine rankings. Here are some advanced link-building strategies to consider:

1. **Create Linkable Assets:** Develop high-quality, link-worthy content that provides unique value to your target audience. Linkable assets such as comprehensive guides, research reports, infographics, and interactive tools are more likely to attract natural backlinks from other websites.

2. **Guest Blogging and Contributorship:** Contribute guest posts to authoritative websites and industry publications in your niche. Guest blogging allows you to showcase your expertise,

build relationships with influencers, and earn valuable backlinks to your website.

3. **Broken Link Building:** Identify broken links on other websites in your niche and reach out to webmasters to suggest replacing them with links to relevant content on your website. Broken link building is a win-win strategy that helps webmasters fix broken links while earning backlinks for your website.

4. **Skyscraper Technique:** Identify popular topics and content in your industry with many backlinks. Create better, more comprehensive, and updated versions of this content, then reach out to websites linking to the original content to suggest linking to your improved version.

Voice Search Optimization

With the rising popularity of voice-enabled devices and virtual assistants like Siri, Alexa, and Google Assistant, voice search optimization has become increasingly important for SEO. Voice search optimization focuses on optimizing your website's content and structure to better align with the way people search using voice commands. Here are some tips for voice search optimization:

1. **Optimize for Featured Snippets:** Featured snippets are concise answers displayed at the top of search results. Optimize your content to answer common questions and queries related to your niche, as featured snippets are often read aloud by voice assistants in response to voice search queries.

2. **Use Natural Language Keywords:** Voice search queries tend to be more conversational and long-tail compared to text-based searches. Optimize your content for natural language keywords and phrases that reflect how people speak and ask questions in everyday language.

3. **Local SEO Optimization:** Many voice searches are local in nature, such as "near me" searches for local businesses and services. Optimize your website for local SEO by including location-

specific keywords, creating local content, and optimizing your Google My Business listing.

4. **Improve Page Load Speed:** Voice search users expect quick and direct answers to their queries. Ensure that your website loads quickly on all devices and provides a seamless user experience to improve your chances of appearing in voice search results.

By implementing advanced SEO techniques such as schema markup implementation, advanced link-building strategies, and voice search optimization, you can further enhance your website's visibility, authority, and performance in search engine results pages (SERPs). These techniques require ongoing optimization and refinement to stay ahead of the competition and adapt to evolving search engine algorithms.

Conclusion

Congratulations on completing "The Beginner's Guide to SEO: Boost Your Website's Visibility"! Throughout this Book, we have covered fundamental concepts, advanced techniques, and common mistakes in SEO to help you understand how to improve your website's visibility in search engine results pages (SERPs). As we conclude, let us recap the key takeaways, provide encouragement to start implementing SEO strategies, and offer resources for further learning.

Recap of Key Takeaways

1. **Understanding SEO Basics:** SEO involves optimizing your website to improve its visibility and rankings in search engine results pages (SERPs). It encompasses various strategies, including keyword research, on-page optimization, off-page optimization, technical SEO, and more.

2. **Importance of Quality Content:** High-quality content is essential for SEO success. Focus on creating valuable, relevant, and engaging content that meets the needs of your target

audience and incorporates targeted keywords naturally.

3. **Optimizing User Experience (UX):** Prioritize user experience in your SEO strategy by optimizing website speed, mobile responsiveness, navigation, and overall usability. Positive user experiences lead to higher engagement and better search engine rankings.

4. **Measuring Success with SEO Metrics:** Track key performance indicators (KPIs) such as organic traffic, keyword rankings, conversion rates, and backlink profile to assess the effectiveness of your SEO efforts and make data-driven decisions.

5. **Avoiding Common SEO Mistakes:** Avoid black hat tactics like keyword stuffing, prioritize mobile optimization, and stay updated on search engine algorithm updates to maintain and improve your website's visibility and rankings.

6. **Implementing Advanced SEO Techniques:** Consider implementing advanced techniques such as schema markup, advanced link-building strategies, and voice search optimization to further enhance your website's visibility and performance in SERPs.

Encouragement to Start Implementing SEO Strategies

Now that you have a solid understanding of SEO principles and strategies, it is time to put your knowledge into action. Do not be intimidated by the complexity of SEO—start by implementing basic optimization techniques and gradually incorporate more advanced strategies as you gain experience and confidence. Remember that SEO is an ongoing process, and consistent effort and optimization are key to long-term success.

Resources for Further Learning

Continuing your education and staying updated on the latest trends and best practices in SEO is essential for success. Here are some resources for further learning:

1. **Online Courses:** Enroll in online courses and certification programs offered by reputable platforms like Coursera, Udemy, and Moz Academy to deepen your understanding of SEO concepts and techniques.

2. **Blogs and Websites:** Follow industry-leading blogs and websites such as Moz, Search Engine Journal, Search Engine Land, and Neil Patel's blog for insightful articles, guides, and updates on SEO trends and strategies.

3. **Forums and Communities:** Join online forums and communities like Reddit's r/SEO and SEO forums on platforms like LinkedIn and Facebook to connect with other SEO professionals, ask questions, and share experiences and insights.

4. **Official Documentation and Guidelines:** Refer to official documentation and guidelines provided by search engines like Google, Bing, and Yahoo for authoritative information on SEO best practices, algorithm updates, and webmaster guidelines.

Remember that SEO is a dynamic and ever-evolving field, so it is essential to stay curious, adaptable, and proactive in your learning journey.

In conclusion, mastering the art of SEO requires dedication, patience, and continuous learning. By applying the principles and strategies outlined in this guide, you can significantly improve your website's visibility, attract more organic traffic, and achieve your online business goals. Do not hesitate to experiment, test, and iterate on your SEO efforts to find what works best for your website and audience. Good luck on your SEO journey, and may your website soar to new heights of success in the digital landscape!

Appendix

In this appendix, we have compiled a glossary of common SEO terms to help you better understand the terminology used throughout this guide. Additionally, we have provided a list of recommended tools and resources to further support your journey in mastering SEO.

Glossary of SEO Terms

1. **SEO (Search Engine Optimization):** The process of optimizing your website to improve its visibility and rankings in search engine results pages (SERPs).

2. **Keywords:** Words or phrases that users enter into search engines to find information related to their query. Keywords are essential for SEO as they help search engines understand the relevance of your content to users' search queries.

3. **Organic Traffic:** Website traffic that originates from unpaid, natural search engine results. Organic traffic is driven by users clicking on search results rather than paid advertisements.

4. **Backlinks:** Links from other websites that point to your website. Backlinks are an important ranking factor in SEO as they signal to search engines that your website is authoritative and trustworthy.

5. **Meta Tags:** HTML tags that provide metadata about a web page. Common meta tags used for SEO include meta titles, meta descriptions, and meta keywords.

6. **SERP (Search Engine Results Page):** The page displayed by search engines in response to a user's search query. SERPs typically include a combination of organic search results, paid advertisements, and other features like featured snippets and knowledge panels.

7. **Anchor Text:** The clickable text of a hyperlink. Anchor text provides context and relevance to the linked page and is an important factor in SEO.

8. **Page Speed:** The time it takes for a web page to load completely. Page speed is a crucial factor in user experience and SEO, as faster-loading pages tend to rank higher in search results.

9. **Bounce Rate:** The percentage of visitors who navigate away from a website after viewing only

one page. A high bounce rate may indicate poor user experience or irrelevant content.

10. **Crawling and Indexing:** The process by which search engines discover, crawl, and index web pages. Crawling refers to the automated process of browsing the web to discover and analyze web pages, while indexing involves storing and organizing the content of web pages in a searchable index.

Recommended Tools and Resources

1. **Google Analytics:** A free web analytics tool provided by Google that offers insights into website traffic, user behavior, and conversion metrics.

2. **Google Search Console:** A free tool provided by Google that helps website owners monitor and maintain their website's presence in Google Search results. It provides valuable data on search performance, indexing status, and site errors.

3. **SEMrush:** A comprehensive SEO toolkit that offers features such as keyword research,

backlink analysis, site auditing, and competitor analysis.

4. **Ahrefs:** A powerful SEO toolset that provides insights into backlink analysis, keyword research, rank tracking, and site auditing.

5. **Moz:** Offers a suite of SEO tools for keyword research, rank tracking, site auditing, and link analysis.

6. **Schema.org:** A collaborative community project that provides structured data markup vocabulary for webmasters. Implementing schema markup can enhance your website's appearance in search results.

7. **Reddit's r/SEO:** An online community where SEO professionals and enthusiasts discuss industry news, strategies, and best practices.

8. **Search Engine Journal:** A leading source for news and information about SEO, PPC, social media, and digital marketing.

9. **Moz Blog:** Offers insightful articles, guides, and resources on SEO, inbound marketing, and content strategy.

These tools and resources can provide valuable insights, guidance, and support as you continue your journey in mastering SEO and optimizing your website for improved visibility and performance in search engine results pages (SERPs). Explore them further to deepen your understanding and stay updated on the latest trends and best practices in SEO

About the Author:

Hi, I'm Pradeep Kumar, a digital marketer with 5 years of experience. I've helped numerous clients succeed through SEO, PPC, and content strategy. This Book, "The Beginner's Guide to SEO: Boost Your Website's Visibility," is my effort to simplify SEO for beginners.

www.ingramcontent.com/pod-product-compliance
Lightning Source LLC
LaVergne TN
LVHW051611050326
832903LV00033B/4460